A
step by step
guide to
COSHH
assessment

Health and Safety Series booklet HSG97

HSE BOOKS

First published 1993
Reprinted with amendments 1999

ISBN 0 7176 1446 8

This guidance is issued by the Health and Safety Executive.
Following the guidance is not compulsory and you are free
to take other action. But if you do follow the guidance you
will normally be doing enough to comply with the law.
Health and safety inspectors seek to secure compliance
with the law and may refer to this guidance as illustrating
good practice.

Contents

Introduction

1   This booklet provides advice and guidance to employers for assessment of their activities under the Control of Substances Hazardous to Health Regulations 1999 (COSHH).

2   It replaces *COSHH Assessments. A step-by-step guide to assessment and the skills needed for it* published by HSE when COSHH was first introduced. The principles of assessment have not changed since COSHH first appeared, but this booklet illustrates them with extensive examples.

3   COSHH does not set out specific requirements for specific circumstances. It sets out a basic system for managing risk to health. The first component of any management is finding out **what the situation is**, the second is deciding **what to do about it**. In relation to risk from exposure to hazardous substances, these are the two purposes of COSHH assessment.

4   The booklet sets out a sequential framework of distinct stages in carrying out assessment. Parts 1-5 describe each stage in detail. It is a suggested framework and there is no reason why employers should not opt for a different sequence. Whatever route is chosen, the same information is required and it is unlikely to be achieved without a systematic approach.

5   The legal requirement is for assessment to be suitable and sufficient. More serious and complex risks require greater consideration to meet this requirement, simpler and lower risk situations will require less. Some of this booklet will be irrelevant to those assessing simple cases, but much more will be relevant for complex or serious risks.

6   In both cases the aim is reliable conclusions on the basis of informed judgement. The examples are intended to show the range in complexity and depth required to achieve this in different circumstances.

7   This booklet is not a pro forma for assessment. There is an infinite variety of work activities and the range of effective ways of combatting risks is equally extensive. Because of this it is impossible to produce a single format for assessment that defines detailed assessment requirements for all circumstances. That does not mean to say that this guidance cannot or should not be used as a checklist of necessary tasks.

8   COSHH is not a bureaucratic exercise. It is about making sure things are done to reduce pain and suffering caused by ill health. Poor assessment that merely collects information may well result in meaningless mountains of paper. However, good assessment, motivated by a constructive desire to know what is going on and the best ways of dealing with problems, can be used not only for reference but also as a plan for identifying action to reduce ill health.

9   Modern legislation places increasing emphasis on the assessment of all workplace health and safety matters; not just hazardous substances. The underlying management principles of COSHH assessment, ie finding out and then deciding what to do, are the same as those for assessment required by other health and safety legislation. In particular, the Management of Health and Safety at Work Regulations 1992 (MHSW), has a wide-ranging requirement for assessment, overlapping a number of existing Regulations including COSHH. An assessment made under COSHH need not be repeated for the purposes of MHSW. But the COSHH assessment and the whole strategy for management of exposure to hazardous substances under COSHH should be integrated with the arrangements made by employers in response to MHSW. The HSE publication HSG65 *Successful Health and Safety Management* sets out a universal strategy for the management of all workplace health, safety and welfare and is particularly relevant in this respect.

10 This booklet should be read in conjunction with the COSHH Regulations, the Approved Codes of Practice relating to COSHH and other relevant Health and Safety Executive publications giving guidance and advice. (A list of relevant publications is given in the References section at the back of this booklet.) Other sources of technical information may need to be referred to, depending on the circumstances. These can come from a variety of sources which are suggested in the text.

Summary of the assessment process

11 The flow diagram on these pages shows the essential structure of COSHH assessment.

12 The starting point is at the top with a logical progression downwards and anti-clockwise through the following five sections.

13 Each stage of the assessment should be completed before going onto the next. At the end of each stage ask yourself if you are genuinely confident about your assessment so far. If you are, go onto to the next stage, if you are not, go back over what you have done. If you are not sure, it may be because you need more help.

14 The five sections correspond to Parts 1-5 of this booklet:

Are hazardous substances likel to be present in the workplace

NO - No further action required

YES - Assessment required

❶ Gather information about the substances, the work and working practice

Decide who will carry out the assessment **18 - ?**

What substances are present or likely to be **26 -**

Identify the hazards they have **28 - 34**

Find out who could be exposed and how **32 -**

Either by seeing which substances occur in particular activities

or seeing which activi involve exposure to particular substance

❷ Evaluate the risks to health

Either on an individual employee basis

or on a group basis **48 - 49**

FIND OUT

- the chance of exposure occurring **51**

- what level of exposure could happen **56 - 65**

- how long the exposure goes on for **56 - 65**

- how often exposure is likely to occur **52 - 55**

CONCLUDE

Either existing and potential exposure pose no significant risk **66 - 68**

or existing and/or potential exposure pose significant risk **69 - 71**

1 gathering information about the substances, the work and the working practices (or finding out what the problems are);

2 evaluating the risks to health (or looking at the problems that are found);

3 deciding what needs to be done;

4 recording the assessment;

5 reviewing the assessment.

15 Each of the boxes in the flow diagram gives a reference to paragraphs containing further information later in the booklet. If you only need to look at a particular aspect of assessment the references show you where to look.

16 It cannot be over-emphasised that the depth of assessment required depends on the complexity and degree of risk. Simple low risk situations will require little, but high risk complex situations need much more attention. It might take one person 2 minutes to assess the risks from using correction fluid in the office. It could take a multidisciplinary team weeks to assess the risks in the factory where it is made.

17 Assessment does not stop at the bottom of the flow diagram. The Regulations require that assessments are reviewed. This means going back to re-examine earlier conclusions, but if those earlier conclusions are still valid it is not necessary to repeat the whole assessment process. The primary purpose of review is to check and, where necessary, amend assessments; not repeat them.

5

Review the assessment

Decide when review is needed
105 - 109, 111

Decide what needs to be reviewed **110**

4

Record the assessment

Decide if it is necessary to record the assessment
Yes   No **101**

if yes, decide what and how much to record **102 - 103**

Decide presentation and format
104

Decide what needs to be done in terms of:

Controlling or preventing exposure
74 - 78, 82, 83 and part 7

Maintaining controls   Using controls
79 - 80   **81**

Monitoring exposure **84 - 88**

Health surveillance **89 - 94**

Information instruction training **95 - 100**

Gathering information about the substances, the work and the working practices

Decide who will carry out the assessment

18   The smaller the organisation, and the less significant the risks seem, the less likely it is that many people will need to be closely involved in the assessment process. With lesser or more easily understandable risks there will be less need for technical expertise in occupational hygiene to complete suitable and sufficient assessments. (But smallness itself is no guarantee that serious or difficult risks will not occur.)

19   As matters become more complex and varied, usually across larger organisations, then more people will need to be involved. This is not just because more work is required but also because the greater variety of situations will usually require a range of different skills and knowledge.

20   Part 6 of this booklet discusses competence needed for assessment in more detail.

21   As the numbers involved increase so does the need for management of their work. Individual responsibilities should be clearly described by the person in charge of the assessment process; and it is important that whoever is in charge can exercise authority delegated to him or her by the employer.

22   For large assessments many employers have successfully used a combination of a central coordinating body and teams reporting back to it with observations and recommendations. The central body can act in:

▢ selecting competent team members;

▢ giving guidance to make sure teams are looking for the right things;

▢ drawing valid conclusions;

▢ monitoring the recommendations they make;

▢ providing a central source of occupational hygiene expertise.

> **A car assembly plant involves many different departments, eg paintshop, stores, body assembly, engine installation, administration etc.**
>
> **Assessment is evidently a substantial exercise and will require the contribution of many different staff.**

A central coordinating committee is set up, headed by the plant general manager. It is charged with reporting to the company personnel director by a certain date with recommendations for action required to comply with COSHH. The committee includes the departmental heads, the company health and safety manager and senior employee representatives.

Each departmental manager then selects a COSHH team for their own areas. Once all the relevant staff have been selected, both they and the central committee attend a one day in-house training course provided by an external health and safety consultancy. This is not intended to turn everyone into experts, but to make them aware of the nature of COSHH and the sort of approach it requires. The central committee then produces a set of guidelines describing how they want the COSHH teams to report back to them. Departmental heads use these to identify with their teams what the problems are and how they think they should be dealt with. This process includes workshop inspections by the team, including the manager. The manager's visible participation is important in showing that management takes the issue seriously. On the other hand, the involvement of more junior staff in the inspection encourages people to say things they might not necessarily repeat to their boss. During this process it is inevitable that some problems will be raised that the team cannot answer. For instance, it may not be possible to tell if a local exhaust plant is actually controlling exposure to an occupational exposure standard. In that case the Department Manager refers back to the health and safety manager on the central committee and the expertise held by his or her department.

Once all teams have completed their surveys and recommendations they are discussed and compiled by the central committee into a single report for presentation to the personnel director.

23   It is important to involve employees in the assessment process. They have the most direct knowledge of how work is carried out. Their information is vital to an employer in order to ensure assessment that reflects work as it really happens, rather than as it should. It also promotes the commitment of employees to precautions established by the assessment.

24   Employee participation can be on an individual or representative basis, but with larger workforces representatives would usually be more appropriate.

25   Where there are safety representatives appointed by recognised trade unions under the Safety Representatives and Safety Committee Regulations 1977, employers have a general duty to consult them on arrangements for measures to ensure the health of employees and on checking the effectiveness of those measures. This includes consultation on the matters covered by COSHH. Similarly, other employees not covered by such representatives must be consulted either directly or indirectly through elected representatives of employee safety, according to the Health and Safety (Consultation with Employees) Regulations 1996.

Identify the substances present or likely to be

26   Substances hazardous to health include: gases, vapours, liquids, fumes, dusts and solids and can be part of a mixture of materials. Consider what micro-organisms may be present (including the egg and larval stages of many parasites).

Find out what substances are coming into the business and where they are used, worked on, handled or stored; all should be accounted for. Check stock lists.

Think what substances might be produced during any process as intermediates, by-products or finished products or what might be given off as wastes, residues, fumes, dusts etc.

Think what might be transported, collected, poured, weighed, packed, discharged or disposed of.

Remember that substances are used in, or arise from maintenance, cleaning, repair work, research or testing laboratories etc.

They can also arise from work on the structure of the building, eg removal of insulating materials or sandblasting during facade cleaning.

How can hazardous substances be recognised?

27   By knowledge of the process and from previous experience.

If substances are bought in to the workplace, by considering the information provided by suppliers.

By checking if the substance is listed in Guidance Note EH40 (this lists substances which have been given occupational exposure standards and maximum exposure limits).

By checking if the substance is defined as a carcinogen in regulation 2.

By checking the approved lists (see References section) to see if the substance falls into any of the classifications in Regulation 2(1)(a) ie toxic, very toxic, corrosive etc.

By reading HSE guidance notes.

By reading relevant trades association and technical literature.

By asking the advice of trades associations, other employers etc or by asking a competent toxicology, occupational hygiene or health adviser.

Note: Suppliers are legally required to provide adequate information; it can take a number of forms, including labels and data sheets. Ask them if it is not provided or if you cannot understand what they have sent you. Advice on the interpretation of suppliers' information is contained in HSE leaflet INDG186 (see References section). Read all the information on labels very carefully.

Office accommodation

Photocopier toner and developer fluids

Domestic cleaning materials:

    bleach

    toilet cleaner

    window cleaner

    furniture polishes

    floor cleaners

Substances found in maintenance

departments:

    paints

    solvents

    biocides

    lubricating oils

Typist correction fluids

Ozone generation from photocopiers

Flysprays, mouse poisons and other

pest control substances

Boat building

Wood dust

Paints

Fibre glass resin (fumes and resin)

Glass resin

Welding fume

Solvents

Diesel and diesel fumes

Varnishes

Adhesives

Pesticides (anti-fouling paints, timber

preservatives etc)

Waterborne diseases, eg leptospirosis)

All the substances found in offices

Identify how the substances are hazardous

28   Think whether each substance is in a form in which it could be:

- inhaled;

- swallowed (either directly or from settling on food etc or from eating food with contaminated fingers);

- absorbed or introduced through the skin or via the eyes (either directly or from contact with contaminated surfaces or clothing);

- injected into the body by high pressure equipment or contaminated sharp objects.

Pesticides:

these substances can enter the body through most routes and there is ample opportunity for them to do so.

Ingestion - smoking/eating/drinking with contaminated hands or face.

Inhalation - operator's (and other persons') exposure to spray drift or vapour during spraying, mixing, adjusting etc.

Absorption - splashes on unprotected skin, especially during tank mixing or filling.

Contact with contaminated clothing, surfaces or recently treated areas.

Swallowing - blowing out blocked nozzles.

Hydrogen sulphide

This gas is encountered in many confined spaces in potentially lethal concentrations. It poses a significant risk through inhalation but is a negligible hazard via other routes. Assessment therefore requires minimal, if any, consideration of those other routes.

29 Check out all forms in which the substance may be present. Some substances can be virtually harmless in some forms (eg as a block of metal) while very hazardous in others (eg the same metal as a dust or fume).

What effects could they have?

30 For each route of entry or contact identified, find out what sort of harm could result (sources of information in paragraph 27 will be useful).

- Could serious effects or death, either immediate or delayed, could occur from single exposures to the substances (ie the effects of acute exposure)?

    Inhaling dangerous concentrations of cadmium fumes (eg when cutting or burning off cadmium coated steel) can result in severe short-term effects. A few hours after the initial exposure, increasingly severe respiratory and fever symptoms can follow and have been fatal in previous cases.

- Could adverse effects or death result from repeated, even low level, exposures over a period of time (ie the chronic exposures)?

    Longer term exposure to cadmium fume and to a lesser extent dust (eg during cadmium battery or pigment manufacture) can adversely affect both the lungs and kidneys. Kidney damage is likely to appear first but continued exposure can result in emphysema-like symptoms.

- Could there be both long-term and short-term effects. Some substances may have only acute effects and some chronic but, as the previous two examples show, others may have both?

- Could cancers occur?

    It is not only in large, specialised chemical plants that carcinogens may be found. Used engine oils and cutting fluids from engineering processes are considered capable of causing cancer, normally due to skin contact. Consequently there is scope for exposure to carcinogens during vehicle repair and at machining operations.

■ Could the substance cause sensitisation or allergic reactions?

> **Glutaraldehyde has been used as a sterilant in hospitals. It is a powerful irritant and those effects are immediately apparent to those exposed to it. It is also a respiratory sensitiser, but the onset of sensitisation is a more subtle process. Those who have been sensitised to it will suffer severe effects on exposure to minute concentrations, much smaller than those necessary to cause irritation.**

■ Could the substance be harmful to the human reproductive process?

> **Pregnant ewes are known to be carriers of a microorganism known as Chlamydia psittaci. It can cause abortion in pregnant women.**

■ In the case of micro-organisms, could they cause infection or could an infected individual infect others?

> **Many people working with animals are at risk of infection with zoonotic diseases such as leptospirosis or Q fever. The risk of infected people passing those diseases to others is fairly small.**
>
> **On the other hand, in hospitals clinical staff may come into contact with extremely dangerous microorganisms such as Hepatitis B. In this case the risk of an exposed individual spreading infection through the workplace is serious. In the same circumstances other diseases such as Rubella or Chicken Pox may not be so immediately life-threatening, but the potential for spread of infection is high.**

(These examples all affect the types of precautions which will need to be taken.)

31 Check the sources of information for indications of any enhanced harmful effects from exposures to mixtures of substances. These can occur if people come into contact with two or more substances, either at the same time or successively. It may be necessary to ask a competent toxicology or health adviser for further details.

> **Some hand cleansing gels can remove fats and natural oils from the skin. This increases the risk of absorption through the skin of hazardous substances. Gels may be suitable for use at the end of shifts, but they should not be used during them.**

Find out who could be exposed and how

32 This can be organised in either one of two ways:

■ take different work activities and look at all the exposures in each or;

■ take different substances and see where exposure to them occurs across different activities.

33 For simpler cases the latter substance based approach may be successful, especially where few substances are involved. But it can be very wasteful in more complicated situations. For instance, automatically looking for a particular substance across many activities is pointless if the substance only occurs in half of them.

34 The activity based approach gives much more scope for grouping assessment into broadly consistent categories. In this way, especially in larger companies, assessment of similar types of work and risk does not need to be repeated. In all but the simplest cases it is recommended that an activity based approach will be more effective and easier to manage than a substance by substance strategy.

> **A very large national utility took the number of hazardous substances it encountered and multiplied it by the number of different types of work activity it undertook. It assumed this was the number of different COSHH assessments it would have to do. The answer was 20 000. After some thought the number of different types of work involving similar types of exposure were established. The answer was 5000. This was still substantial, which was not surprising taking into account the size of the company, but was vastly more manageable than the numbers based on a substance by substance approach.**

Divide the work up into manageable chunks

35 Careful thought at this stage can save much effort in producing a satisfactory assessment. Hasty assessment will almost certainly result in unnecessary and wasted effort. Some forethought will enable similar types of risk to be identified and conclusions drawn for one area are often, with minor amendment, applicable to others as well. Initial thinking will also make the relative priorities for assessment clearer. Obviously some matters will require more urgent consideration than others.

36 Divide the work into logical units in relation to the substances that are being worked with, eg departments, processes, different groups of people, different locations. Look at each of the units on its own. Walking through the workplace and looking at floor or process plans should help with this division.

> **A school could be divided into the following categories for COSHH assessment**
>
> **Maintenance**   **- grounds**   **- chemical application (including pesticides)**
>   **- exposure to leptispira**
>   **- buildings**   **- water treatment/heating**
>   **- painting**
>   **- woodworking**
>   **- construction**
>   **- cleaning**
>   **- supplying and installing substances**
>   **- swimming pool (chlorine system)**
>   **- pesticide storage**
>   **- pest control**

Teaching	- technical subjects	- science
		- design and technology
	- non technical	- general classroom (minimal concern)
Administration	- general office procedures	

37   If the work involves large numbers of substances, eg research laboratories, group substances on the basis of their properties and the way they are used or handled. It will often be unnecessary to assess each individual chemical in its own right as opposed to assessment of a category. (Identification, through COSHH assessment of what actually is on the premises, can generate large financial savings by drawing attention to wasteful purchasing policies.)

In a laboratory:

◆   acids and bases could be considered in terms of pH banding;

◆   solvents and other generic classes could be grouped into different label descriptions, eg toxic, very toxic;

◆   substances stored in large quantities require their own handling procedures and could be treated separately from smaller stocks;

◆   treating all substances within a group in the same way as the most hazardous one is usually a valid approach. On a fruit farm a particularly wide range of pesticides may be used;

◆   herbicides, insecticides and fungicides could be treated separately;

◆   powder, granular and liquid formulations are easily identifiable and pose different handling problems;

◆   different chemicals may be applied in different ways, eg knapsack sprayer, ground application, foliar application.

Find out who is doing what and what does and could really happen

38   Think of all groups of people, from among:

▢   production employees

▢   ancillary or support-services employees
(Note: Cleaners and maintenance staff are often exposed not only to substances from their own activities, but to those from production activities as well.)

▢   contractors on site

▢   visitors

▢   supervisors and managers

▢   students

▢   office workers

■ people outside

Retail garden centre with a small facility for manufacturing garden furniture

Full time workers could be exposed to the following:

◆ spillage during handling of garden chemicals;

◆ wood dust, paints, solvents, preservatives and adhesives in the furniture workshop;

◆ forklift diesel fumes in storage buildings;

◆ dipping bulbs with organophosporous pesticide.

Ancillary workers could be exposed to the following:

◆ cleaners mopping up spillages;

◆ cleaners using hazardous cleaning materials, eg bleach;

◆ maintenance workers repairing contaminated racking.

Contractors and visitors (including the public), could be exposed to a variety of hazards, especially where there is little supervision or control of access to various parts of the premises.

Supervisors and managers are likely to be exposed to all the circumstances listed, although it will usually be of greatly reduced length and intensity.

Students and other casual workers might be employed to stack shelves. There is some scope for them to come into contact with spillages of hazardous substances in this work. They may also find themselves helping out in other areas when there is a temporary need for an 'extra hand'.

Office workers will be exposed to the normal range of substances found in offices. They may also have incidental contact with other work activities on the site. For instance, do they regularly have to pass through the woodworking shop to get to the office?

There will usually be little scope for effects on people outside the premises, but instances where there is might include:

◆ spray drift from pesticide treatment of outside plants;

◆ disposal of spent bulb treatment solution;

◆ fumigation of on-site production (as opposed to display) glasshouses.

39 Look at what the people in each group are doing and how. People do not always work 'by the book' and they may devise their own methods. This does not mean that shop floor practices are always wrong and some of the most elegantly simple solutions can be derived from workers' ideas. Remember the point of assessment is real solutions that work in practice for the problems in individual workplaces.

Welders often have to approach their workpieces from different angles. As the fume always rises, exposure can vary greatly depending on the position of the welder relative to it. Local exhaust ventilation with movable capture hoods is available to cope with this problem. However, where it is provided many operators fail to move the hood as they alter their position; consequently the LEV is rendered largely ineffective.

Although it is well known in the printing industry that carrying solvent rags in coverall pockets results in gross skin contamination, it still goes on.

On the other hand, workers may have modified empty containers as simple and convenient storage bins for rags at the places where they are needed. (Good ideas generated from the shop floor are more likely to be taken up enthusiastically than imposition from management. This emphasises the need for employees to be involved in the assessment process.)

40   Ask what happens to working practices when events such as cleaning, breakdowns, sudden staff shortages, changes in personnel, changes in the volume of production and adverse weather conditions occur. (These can all have a great effect on whether and to what extent people are exposed to substances.)

Construction and agricultural employees working outdoors may well be tempted to discard protective coveralls and other personal protective equipment (PPE) during hot weather. This illustrates the reasons for the 'last resort' status of PPE under COSHH and the need for careful selection to suit the user and circumstances when it is used.)

During the peak harvesting season a food processing factory may employ additional casual labour and operate a multi-shift system. Casual labour will not have the same appreciation of what precautionary measures are required and during late shifts there is likely to be less comprehensive management control of what is going on.

Local exhaust ventilation is an essential control method in numerous applications. It is essential that defects are repaired as soon as possible, but this is not always the case, especially where shortcomings are not reported.

A chemical process relies on the mixing of two components fed into a reaction vessel at a constant rate. Because of an intermittently leaky flange in the pipeline supplying one of the components the reaction often slows down. Does the operator increase the flow (and thus the rate of contamination from the leak) or stop to repair the leak? (Why has the leak not been properly repaired in the first place?)

Note any differences between people in a group

41   Consider separately anyone whose working habits, size, working posture or personal hygiene practices (eg washing, eating) are significantly different. This also applies to anyone who

might possibly have increased susceptibility to the effects of substances, eg young persons, those known to be sensitised to specific substances, those with chronic bronchitis.

42 Remember the less 'visible' ancillary people, such as cleaners, maintenance personnel, research and development staff, crane drivers, storekeepers, contractors, visitors etc.

> **A large feed mill employs sales representatives as well as production personnel. They are likely to have daily exposure as they walk through the mill buildings for morning and evening meetings with the sales manager. This could be particularly important where there are any signs of sensitisation to grain dust. Probably more importantly, they visit a wide range of industrial, warehouse and business premises during their working day. They need to have an awareness of the risks to health they may encounter and how to react to them.**

> **Local authority engineers may have to enter sewers where there is a risk of fatal gassing. In these circumstances full, self-contained breathing apparatus would be essential. If the wearer has a beard there will be a poor fit of the face mask which could have fatal consequences.**

> **Vets sometimes use powerful tranquillisers to sedate large animals such as deer and horses. These substances are fatal to humans in very small amounts. Their use demands responsibility and non-complacency by vets and their assistants.**

> **To get away quickly after work, some workers may prefer to keep their own coats hung up at their work station rather than in separate lockers. Consequently the coat becomes contaminated and the worker receives additional exposure from wearing it; and also takes it home to his or her family.**

> **Loading stone into wagons at quarries is usually undertaken by high capacity loader shovels. Dust levels can be dramatically reduced by minimising drop heights from the bucket to the wagon. However, drivers often get into the habit of doing the exact opposite.**

Sources of information

43 Follow best practices from the outset to avoid subsequent expensive modifications. Read relevant HSE and industry association codes of practice and guidance. Collect information from potential suppliers of substances and plant.

44 Ask other employers in similar processes and trades associations for their advice and experiences.

45 Discuss with employees' representatives.

46 As the equipment is installed, gather information from 'trial runs' if feasible. Where appropriate, simulate breakdowns, emergencies etc and adjust plans as necessary.

47 Base the assessment on what happens at the commissioning stage, so that any deficiencies can be identified and put right.

Evaluating the risks to health

Decide whether you will evaluate risks to groups or individuals

48 COSHH requires precautions to be taken for the protection of every employee. However, in many cases, the risks to each individual can be reliably determined by considering groups with the same or similar working characteristics and concentrating on a few people who are representative and typical of each group.

> **In a factory producing televisions, circuit boards are assembled on production lines. At each stage in the line a number of workers carry out identical work. In that case it is not necessary to assess individual exposures to arrive at reliable conclusions for all the members of a group.**

> **Different fitters employed by a contract maintenance company may visit a wide range of premises involving different exposures and risks. In that case it will be difficult to draw single conclusions appropriate to the different fitters and assessment will be required on an individual employee basis.**

49 Working out the risk involves combining the answers to the following questions:

- What is the potential of a substance for causing harm (ie the hazard)?

- What is the chance of exposure occurring?

- How often is exposure liable to occur?

- How much are people exposed to and for how long?

What is the potential of a substance for causing harm?

50 For the substances which have been identified as arising in the course of any work, harmful potential should already be apparent from having completed Part 1.

What is the chance of the exposure occurring?

51 Consider the following questions in relation to the information collected about the work in Part 1. Also bear in mind the various ways in which harmful exposures can occur. People can come into contact with a substance if they:

- work with it directly;

- are in the vicinity of where it is handled, transported, used, worked upon, collected, packed, stored, disposed of, discharged or given off etc; or is simply present in the environment;

> **A textile company uses reactive dyes which are potent respiratory sensitisers requiring high standards of control. As well as those working directly with the powders the following are also potentially exposed and the risks to them need to be assessed:**
>
> **dyestuff storekeeper; maintenance staff working on contaminated LEV; cleaners; workers adjacent to weighing and mixing stations.**

- are in the vicinity of an accidental release or spillage;

> **A warehouse routinely stores large quantities of hazardous substances. Handling with fork-lift trucks inevitably involves some breakage of containers ranging from single package leaks to spillage of entire pallet loads. Staff come into contact with the substances both through clearing the spillage and the general need to move about the warehouse.**

- enter an enclosed space where it might be present;

> **Exposure to Trichlorethylene during routine use of a large degreasing tank may be adequately controlled. However, entry into the tank for maintenance and cleaning purposes entails life-threatening risks and requires very stringent standards of control. Alternative working methods that do not involve tank entry may be reasonably practicable and these should always be the first option.**

- disturb deposits of the substance on surfaces (eg during cleaning) and make them airborne;

> **Local exhaust ventilation in a chrome plating works may require regular maintenance and cleaning, which will often disturb deposits of caked chromic acid. Therefore maintenance workers will almost inevitably be exposed at very close hand to high concentrations of dust.**

- wear previously contaminated clothing or protective equipment;

> **Agricultural workers should wear respiratory protection when shovelling material in feed lofts. The RPE is commonly hung on a nail in the loft for easy access. Since the loft is normally filled pneumatically the RPE will be heavily contaminated and rendered useless, becoming a source of exposure, rather than protection against it.**

■ come into contact with contaminated surfaces;

> **A lorry driver operates a tanker carrying a corrosive substance. During filling through the top hatches there is spillage down the side of the tank and onto the trailer chassis. The driver is liable to come into contact with the substance as he prepares the trailer for travel.**

■ have the substance passed on to them from someone else, eg from other people's contaminated clothing or from personal contact.

> **A laboratory arranges for employee overalls to be cleaned by an industrial laundry. At the end of each shift workers place their overalls in a bin and they are subsequently collected by cleaning staff. The cleaning staff are at risk of contamination.**

How often is exposure liable to occur?

52 Judge from general knowledge and experience of the type of work and information supplied by workpeople and their representatives.

53 Consider, in particular, people and activities where exposure is routinely very frequent (eg virtual daily exposure).

54 Consider the consequences of any non-routine work, production of one-off items or isolated batches, trials, maintenance, repair operations, spillages etc.

55 Remember, when planning work, that the chances of harmful exposures occurring are often linked to:

■ the training and information given to employees, including supervisors;

■ the reliability and suitability of the existing control measures for the job and the people engaged in it; and

■ the quality of the maintenance of the control measures.

> **Loading road tankers with concentrated sulphuric acid at a chemical factory is a high priority for COSHH assessment.**
>
> **The filling operation is normally carried out by company drivers who have been comprehensively trained in the correct procedures.**
>
> **It is also common that independent contract tankers driven by non company staff are filled. These drivers are often unfamiliar with standard filling procedures. In addition it is often difficult to achieve a good seal between contractor tank hatches and site filling equipment, increasing the likelihood of spills.**
>
> **Because the acid is corrosive there is a heavy maintenance burden. Fitters frequently have to work on heavily contaminated plant.**

What levels are people exposed to and how long for?

56 The pattern and total time of exposure during the entire work period can usually be determined by observing and asking the people concerned.

57 It is not always necessary to carry out measurements for COSHH assessments. The aim is to identify what needs to be done. In many cases it will be obvious that conditions are satisfactory without measuring them. For instance, a process completely sealed inside a well maintained enclosure is unlikely to cause significant exposure to those outside it but if particularly hazardous subsances are involved measurement would be appropriate to confirm the situation and the exposure of maintenance workers will be significant. The workplace may also comply with all the detailed conditions specified in HSE and other literature that in practice will achieve adequate control. If those standards are achieved there is less benefit to be gained from carrying out measurements.

58 As certainty about the levels of exposure declines, the need for their measurement will increase. Always err on the side of caution and measure where significant doubt exists. Measurement identifies the scale of a problem so that an appropriate response can be made. It is valuable for avoiding both under- and over-reaction.

59 An indication of the amount or concentration of exposure can often be given by simple tests (eg indicator tubes, dust lamps).

60 Sometimes the amount cannot be established with confidence without taking detailed measurements. If there is still doubt, be on the safe side in deciding on precautions later.

61 Always take into account the conditions or circumstances which could be expected to give rise to the greatest exposures.

62 It is especially important to know precisely about the amount or concentration and length of time of exposure when:

■ exposure occurs routinely very frequently;

■ a high level of exposure can be foreseen at any time;

■ a substance has a maximum exposure limit or an occupational exposure standard, or is a carcinogen, or is known to be particularly hazardous.

63 Advice on sampling for airborne contaminants is contained in the HSE publication *Monitoring strategies for toxic substances* HSG173.

64 In the case of substances hazardous by ingestion or absorption through the skin, biological monitoring (ie measuring bodily uptake by analysing biological samples, eg of blood and urine) may be needed.

65 There should be standards against which the results can be compared: eg maximum exposure limits, occupational exposure standards, biological exposure levels.

A woodworking premises producing high quality reproduction furniture.

Workers may be employed as joiners, cabinet makers or similarly specific job titles. However, in reality employees are much more likely to undertake a variety of tasks outside these traditional divisions. Assessment will not reflect real life if strict demarcation of job content is assumed. The assessor needs to find out who actually does what.

Dust generation is a universal consequence of most woodworking businesses. It can include exposure to hardwood dust which is carcinogenic. Where no control measures are in place it may not need personal monitoring to conclude that exposure levels are unacceptable. Where local exhaust ventilation is installed the question may well be "Is it performing adequately?". Performance can only be ensured by proper design and maintenance. Simple dust lamp techniques can quickly highlight failures.

Where organic solvents and adhesives are used, often characteristic odours are likely to pervade the premises, but this does not necessarily indicate inadequate exposure control. Usually smell is not a very good guide to judging concentrations in air, even though it is an indispensable aid to walkthrough surveys. For more accurate assessment, data from use of simple indicator tubes is often effective.

Exposure to the same organic compounds may involve complicated patterns. For instance, different types of furniture may involve more or less use of adhesives or more or less volatile substances may be used. In that case more extensive investigation than a simple 'one off' indicator tube survey may be required to establish the real state of affairs confidently.

Where there is obviously gross exposure, eg substantial dust deposits, dust hanging visibly in the air, vapour to the point of physical discomfort; it is not necessary for measurement to conclude that control is inadequate, but is to find out how inadequate.

The amount and nature of dust given off during sanding may vary considerably because of, for instance:

♦ type of wood;

♦ coarseness of sanding;

♦ the number of machines in operation.

The maximium potential for exposure, rather than just the usual, should be considered.

There are a number of substances likely to be found in furniture making that are subject to occupational exposure limits; in particular the following are subject to maximum exposure limits:

hardwood and softwood dusts;

1.1.1-trichlorethane (adhesives);

dichloromethane (paint strippers and some adhesives);

isocyanates (2 pack polyurethane paints and varnishes);

2 ethoxy ethanol solvent (some stains and lacquers);

formaldehyde (given off during the machining of particle board).

Adequate control for these substances requires that the specified levels are not exceeded, and in the case of MELs reduced to as low a level as reasonably practicable. The assessment should be able to show that this is achieved. If the highest standards of control, for example those specified in HSE guidance, have been implemented and are working properly, it can be reasonable to assume adequate control. But in other cases the same confidence cannot be assumed. In those cases some form of air sampling or exposure monitoring may be necessary to establish whether there is compliance with the requirement for adequate control.

Draw conclusions about the risks to health

When might there be grounds for concluding exposure is not a risk to health?

66   Sometimes, even without taking measurements, there are reasonable grounds for reaching this conclusion, eg:

▪ quantities or rate of use of the substance are too small to constitute a risk under foreseeable circumstances of use, even if controls broke down;

> A certain small office photocopier sited in a separate room generates ozone. Natural ventilation is relied upon to disperse the gas. The instructions to staff recommend that the window is left open but it may be closed, especially in winter. However, the general ventilation system still guarantees movement of air and this is sufficient to disperse ozone. (Note that while this may be the case for incidental use of this type of photocopier, it may not be so for a photocopying room, where staff are exposed to day long ozone generation from a number of constantly working machines.)

▪ operations are strictly in accordance with well documented information provided about the process and operating conditions by the suppliers of the plant, in which they give a valid assurance that the operation will not give rise to risks to health;

> A small garage enterprise expands from mechanical work into a full accident repair business. As part of this it installs a fully equipped, purpose-built ventilated

> spraying booth and employs a fully qualified vehicle paint sprayer with longstanding experience. The supplying company is well known as a market leader in designing and installing equipment that minimises the risks to operators. Their service includes a comprehensive planning of the installation taking into account the implications of hazardous substances used. As part of the package they provide a comprehensive on-site training course for the operator and employer, which addresses health and safety matters in depth. There is no need for the employer to repeat this work in his assessment, but his assessment will need to refer to the operating documents from the supplier.

■ previous measurements have been taken of the process, in-house or elsewhere, including 'worst case' situations, which confirm that exposure is not a risk to health at any time, and conditions now are demonstrably still the same;

■ the process is conducted exactly to the same standards, or better, as in up-to-date HSE, Industry Advisory Committee, Subject Advisory Committee or industry association guidance on good practice, that carries valid assurance of insignificant exposure.

> The air conditioning system in a large office block includes wet cooling towers situated on the roof. There is an obvious hazard from Legionella. A senior management decision is made to follow to the letter the advice and guidance contained in the HSC Approved Code of Practice and the HSE guidance on the control of Legionellosis. Management systems are established to implement and sustain the procedures and standards described in the code and guidance.

Remember

67　While routine, day-to-day, exposure may not constitute a risk to health (eg with an enclosed system), the failure of the control measures could result in serious risks (eg the system releasing its contents). The assessment must address these risks and the precautions to prevent them happening.

> Routine operator exposure to flour dust is minimised by a system where all milling operations are carried out in sealed enclosures and transfer of flour is carried out pneumatically in a closed system. The assessment does not address the potential for leakage from the pneumatic system. Since no clear arrangements exist for dealing with leaks high exposures are quickly encountered as a result of flour dust being liberated under considerable pressure.

68　Do not dismiss the risks as negligible unless there is certain and valid evidence to be able to do so. In all other cases, there are risks to health from exposure which must be identified and which must trigger precautions to protect people's health.

When might exposure constitute a risk to health?

69   Unacceptable risks to health exist if exposure is known or found to be;

- occurring in situations where it is reasonably practicable for it to be prevented; or

- inadequately controlled in relation to the priorities set out in COSHH Regulation 7. (In particular, exposure to carcinogens must, if it cannot be prevented, be controlled by a combination of inherently more effective control strategies.)

(In either situation, immediate corrective action is required.)

70   The following are examples of immediate indicators where exposure is very likely to constitute a risk to health and to require investigation and remedial action:

- evidence of fine deposits on people or surfaces;

> **Dust on surfaces in a foundry fettling shop, even where ventilated booths are fitted and fan motors appear to be operating normally. Is there leakage from ventilation ducting?**

- fumes or particles visible in the air (eg in light beams);

> **Aerosols generated at chrome plating baths.**

- broken, clearly defective or badly maintained control measures;

> **Heavily contaminated respiratory protection;**
> **deformed local exhaust extractor hoods;**
> **leaking enclosures.**

- an absence of, or departure from, recognised good practice. Such poor performance is as likely to be a result of poor management supervision as it is employee intransigence;

> **Eating, drinking and smoking on the factory floor;**
> **personal protective equipment that never needs to be replaced as it is never used;**
> **unauthorised entry into restricted areas.**

- complaints of discomfort or excessive odour. These are often channelled through employee representatives and should be taken seriously, especially in situations where management staff have less direct contact with the shop floor;

> **An employee at a water treatment works complains of a smell of rotten eggs. His line manager dismisses it as one of the things you have to get used to in the job. In fact it arises from a dangerous build up of hydrogen sulphide in a confined space to which regular access is required.**

■ if ill health linked to exposure has been reported or detected during health surveillance. Health surveillance can vary from simple questions from trained supervisors to full blown medical supervision. It is important that equal importance is attached to adverse reports from all types of health surveillance.

71 The following are examples of exposures that could present increased future risks to health and they are all reasonably foreseeable:

■ undetected deterioration in performance of control measures;

> A contract crop sprayer relies on cab filtration for protection during spraying. Renewal of the filters is forgotten and exposure progressively increases as their performance inevitably declines.

■ plant or system failure;

> A transport company stores drums of chemicals in transit at its main depot. Inside the drum the substances pose little risk. However, the drums are poorly stacked five high and there will be gross contamination if or when they fall.

■ failure to use control measures properly;

> In a plastics factory fumes from hot cutting are controlled by a combination of local exhaust ventilation and operation at lower temperatures. The operator increases the temperature above what is necessary for efficient cutting. As a result more fumes are produced than the ventilation can cope with efficiently.

■ human error, through lack of awareness;

> At a large nursery temporary seasonal labour is taken on to bunch and pack daffodils. The workers are not made aware of the potential for the plant sap to cause severe contact dermatitis. As a result they do not wear the protective gloves that are provided.

■ changes in methods of work.

> Because they are cheaper a small photographic business switches to buying developing fluids in bulk. As a result developing involves an extra process when fluid is decanted from large to small containers. Room for storage is cramped, access is awkward and there is clear potential for operator contamination from spillage etc.

Deciding on the necessary measures to comply with Regulations 7 to 12 of COSHH

72 At this stage assessment should have reached decisions on what the problems are. The next stage is to decide what is to be done about them. Complete the assessment by considering the precautions that are necessary in the light of the risks. If the risks are significant now or could foreseeably become so, then further precautions are required.

73 Not all problems can be solved immediately and priorities for action will be required. Deciding priorities involves a mixture of the following;

- what are the most serious risks to health?

- what are the risks that are likely to occur soonest?

- what are the risks that can be dealt with soonest?

The most important of these is the seriousness of the risk. If a risk is serious it should be dealt with immediately. Less important matters should not assume greater priority merely because they can be dealt with more easily or occur more quickly.

Selection of measures to prevent or control exposure

74 This guidance does not describe the full range of exposure prevention and control strategies available. These are discussed in a number of other HSE publications (see References section).

75 As a rule, if exposure cannot be prevented, the most effective and reliable strategies should be used wherever feasible. COSHH places emphasis on controlling exposure at its source, for example, by using enclosures, hoods, local exhaust ventilation etc, because these methods are inherently more effective than personal protective equipment (PPE). However PPE, including respiratory protective equipment, may be needed when it is not reasonably practicable to control exposure at its source, or such methods are inadequate and it is not reasonably practicable to achieve adequate control by improving their performance.

76 Examples in part 7 of this guide discuss the basis for selecting different prevention and/or control measures in more detail.

77 Taking advice from specialists may save money in the long run, rather than prolonged trial and error; especially with more technically demanding aspects such as ventilation plant.

78 Trade association publications, HSE guidance notes etc may provide useful ideas.

Maintaining control measures

79 Subsequent maintenance commitments should also influence choice of methods. Do not select any controls for which there are not enough resources or expertise to keep them going properly.

> A large rural local authority employs numerous grass and hedge cutter operators for maintaining roadside verges. The employees are widely dispersed, working in small teams from several workshop premises. Machinery repairs, for which there is a frequent need, are carried out by machine operators in the outlying workshops. A widespread exposure to welding fumes has been identified. Reliable operation of ventilated welding booths across all the workshops would be difficult to guarantee. The operators are principally machine drivers and are less competent as maintenance staff. More rather than less supervision is necessary with regard to welding, but this is difficult to achieve for a widely dispersed workforce.
>
> Instead of installing booths at each workshop and attempting to train and supervise, the local authority decides to employ, train and equip a mobile fitter.

80 Personal protective equipment, especially respiratory protection, needs a big back-up in training, supervision and maintenance etc if it is to provide the intended level of protection. Incorrect choice, fitting or insufficient use can render it ineffective.

> A large fruit orchard has no alternative but to follow an intensive programme of tree canopy spraying. To date this has been undertaken using conventional tractors and trailed sprayers. That method involves a lot of airborne contamination. Much reliance has to be placed on personal protective equipment while the spraying is going on. The PPE becomes badly contaminated and needs frequent cleaning and renewal. Because of this, effective management of the PPE regime is a difficult task. There have been frequent occasions where supplies of replacement filters for respirators have run out. As a result it is known that respirators are commonly worn when the condition of the filters is in some doubt. In addition there are two sprayer operators and one is known to be less conscientious over the proper use of PPE.
>
> The employer decides to replace the existing system with a specialised self-propelled, orchard spraying machine. This incorporates an environmentally controlled cab which effectively prevents operator exposure, negating the need for PPE during spraying (but not during mixing, cleaning etc). It also has the major advantage of being purpose-built for the task and dramatically improves the timeliness of spray application.

Making sure control measures are used

81 Essential in virtually every case are:

■ arrangements to ensure that all control measures are properly and fully used. The clear allocation of managerial responsibilities and accountabilities is particularly important in this respect;

> The job description for a steel rolling mill production manager specifies that at monthly intervals he reports to the general manager on the state of compliance with control measures specified in the COSHH assessment. This supplements the minimum requirements of the Regulations for 14-monthly testing and examination of ventilation equipment.

> The design of some control measures can be arranged to encourage their use. For instance, a movable exhaust hood for welding is more likely to be used closer to the work, if the lighting necessary is attached to it. If turning the light on automatically turns on the fan that too will promote more consistent use of the ventilation.

- periodic checks and arragements to make sure that any defects in control measures are reported and put right promptly;

> A hat factory uses local exhaust ventilation to remove solvent fumes given off from racks of drying hats. The racks are moved to the LEV which is fixed and positioning of the racks is important in achieving adequate exposure control. Moving the racks is usually carried out by relatively unskilled labour. Without the ventilation, solvent fumes build up very quickly to dangerous levels and this is not helped by the process being sited in an older building where good quality general ventilation is difficult to achieve. For these reasons it is particularly important that the exhaust ventilation is working at peak efficiency.

> To ensure this happens supervisors are instructed to check the performance and proper use of ventilation daily. Employees are trained in the correct techniques for positioning the racks. In addition placards are displayed clearly at the LEV describing the indications of poor performance. The placards also instruct employees that if any of those indications are noted they must be reported to a named supervisor. The supervisor is under instruction to respond to any reports as soon as possible and has been given the authority, by senior management, to require the maintenance engineer to carry out any necessary repairs or adjustments.

- arrangements for maintenance of all measures, which includes timetables and schedules for periodic examination and test of engineering controls and items of respiratory protective equipment. It is one thing for somebody to realise that something is or may go wrong, it is another for action to be taken to repair or prevent the problem occurring;

> Local exhaust ventilation is installed at the bagging off point of a portland cement plant. Management arrangements are described in the assessment for ensuring that it is examined and tested at appropriate intervals. In order to ensure that those

arrangements are enacted large stickers are fixed at the workstations each time examination and tests are carried out. The stickers state that bagging is not permitted after a certain date; that date being when the next test or examination is due. Providing the tests and examinations are carried out in time the 'cut off' date will always be in the future. The success of this approach will depend on the real authority of workers not to use the equipment beyond the expiry date. That is of course dependent on the real level of management commitment to the aims of COSHH.

■ systems for keeping records of examinations and tests. COSHH requires that these are kept for at least five years. The aim is not to produce records' for records sake. They demonstrate that legal requirements have been carried out, but they also have a useful role to play in examining the effectiveness of control measures; especially during assessment review.

There is no stipulation of the type of recording system required. For many employers, especially in smaller businesses, simple formats such as a single book will suffice. For more complex situations more sophisticated techniques will be necessary, and computer systems offer particular scope. Some companies offer ready-made COSHH data recording packages, both paper and electronically based. For many employers (and in particular larger ones) these can be very helpful.

Plan for emergencies

82 If it is still reasonably foreseeable that leaks, spills or other uncontrolled releases of a hazardous substance could occur, decide on the means for limiting the extent of the risks and for regaining control as quickly as possible.

83 The following aspects are particularly relevant in planning for emergency actions:

■ people and equipment available to minimise quantities released and to contain what has been lost;

■ emergency procedures and training;

■ safe methods for disposal of the substance and contaminated clothing etc;

■ sufficient suitable personal protective equipment and planned working procedures, so that repairs can be made;

■ means for decontamination of skin and personal protective equipment.

A factory process generates large quantities of a corrosive waste substance, which is removed from holding tanks at regular intervals by disposal contractors' road tankers. The tank outlets are fitted with valves that close automatically on release of the pipe. However, the tankers are not always similarly equipped and it is foreseeable that premature movement of the tanker could result in detachment of the hose with major spillage as a result.

To cater for this event a holding bund is constructed around the loading area to stop spillage spreading. The bund volume exceeds the combined capacity of the holding tank and largest road tanker used. No loading is permitted to take place unless the tanker is within the holding area.

If spillage occurs, controlling it and subsequently clearing it will involve close operator contact with the substance. A high standard of protective clothing will be required which must be readily available and well maintained. Comprehensive washing facilities will be required to clean heavily contaminated clothing after use.

The bund may control the spread but thought also needs to be given to how the spillage will be removed. That might involve the use of emergency pumps and pipelines to transfer the spillage back into the holding tanks.

It is essential that whoever is in charge of the loading procedure knows exactly what to do in an emergency. Only fully trained operators are permitted to carry out the loading task. Outside tanker drivers are prohibited from doing it themselves.

Monitoring exposure

84   Monitoring the exposure of employees to hazardous substances will be required in certain cases and the need for this must be considered in assessment.

85   Monitoring the exposure of employees to a substance is not the same as measuring the amount in the environment. The latter can give information on the likely sources of exposure which can be very useful in helping to identify the priorities for control measures. But measuring environmental levels does not necessarily measure the amount that is actually breathed in or absorbed and it is this which determines the risk of ill health occurring. Environmental measurements can add to exposure monitoring but not replace it.

At an animal feed mill, large quantities of dust are generated inside a crop drier. The dust is extracted by high capacity fans to an enclosed dump box at the rear of the installation. Measuring the levels of dust that are generated inside the drier or the dump box bears no relevance to exposure of the drier operators. However, the extraction system is not 100% effective in removing all dust to the dump box and operators are exposed to this residue. How much they are exposed to depends on where they are working in relation to different emission sources, eg the discharge point is much dustier than the control panel. It also depends on how long they work in those different places. The employer is not sure if operator exposure to dust is adequately controlled and so assessment includes measurements of personal exposure. They show excessive exposure. Environmental measurements are then taken to identify the areas where the largest emissions occur. This is combined with knowledge about how long operators work near to different emissions. Better decisions can then be made about which ones need to be more tightly controlled in order to achieve adequate exposure control.

25

86   The legal requirement for exposure monitoring is given in Regulation 10 and Schedule 5 of the Regulations. Authoritative advice on its interpretation is contained in the COSHH Approved Codes of Practice. In essence, monitoring is required when:

- either the consequences of a failure in control are severe, eg where failure would lead to particularly large exposures or exposures to a particularly hazardous substance;

- or you cannot otherwise be genuinely confident that adequate control is being achieved.

87   Monitoring should not be done purely for monitoring's sake. Numbers on their own contribute little to the management of occupational ill health. When setting up a monitoring regime it should be established what results will indicate a satisfactory state of affairs and what will not. Where substances have been assigned Maximum Exposure Limits (MEL) or Occupational Exposure Standards (OES) this will be easier to establish. Where an OES or MEL does not exist 'in-house' standards should be developed if exposure monitoring is carried out.

88   The action that results from adverse results should also be specified. This may be review of the assessment, as adverse results could indicate that the arrangements for achieving control specified in the assessment are not valid, or are not being properly implemented. Adverse results should certainly prompt a check that the existing measures are operating as specified in the assessment.

> A pharmaceutical factory uses hormonal ingredients in its products. Assessment has derived in-house exposure limits for which there is reasonable confidence that control to those levels will prevent adverse health effects. Control is achieved through a high standard of exhaust ventilation at mixing stations. The ventilation is subject to an effective and rigorous testing and examination regime. However, the amounts required to produce ill effect are very small and there is little overt sign of control failure when the limit is exceeded. Exposure monitoring is introduced in order to gain 'real time' data that can usefully indicate compliance with the required standards or otherwise. If adverse results are noted the first response is to check that the ventilation is working as specified; if it is, the initial assessment specifications will then be reviewed.

Health surveillance

89   Health surveillance is required in certain cases: see Regulation 11, Schedule 6 and the Approved Codes of Practice.

90   As with exposure monitoring it is a selective requirement and the need is dependent on the individual circumstances. The primary criterion for this is a reasonable likelihood that the disease or ill-effect associated with exposure will occur in the workplace concerned.

91   Just because there is some exposure does not mean to say that health surveillance is automatically required. If assessment is able to conclude confidently that control measures will prevent the occurrence of adverse effects, then there is little to be gained through

health surveillance. However, as confidence in assessment conclusions declines, then the need for health surveillance will become progressively more important.

92   If it is concluded that health surveillance is necessary, then the form it will take can vary considerably, from simple record keeping to the full participation of doctors in planned surveillance regimes. In general, the greater the likelihood of adverse effects and the more serious their nature, the more sophisticated necessary surveillance will be.

93   Consult a competent occupational health adviser in any cases of uncertainty. (In case of difficulty in obtaining advice, contact the Employment Medical Advisory Service at HSE local offices.)

Sheep dipping contractors are often routinely exposed to organophosphorous (OP) compounds in dip preparations. OP compounds can accumulate insidiously in the body, effecting the nervous system through depression of cholinesterase levels. Symptoms range in seriousness from irritability to respiratory failure. For contractors the frequency of exposure makes ill-effects much more likely. In these cases surveillance involving testing by suitably trained personnel for depression of cholinesterase levels in blood and plasma is essential and required by COSHH.

Cutting oils used in engineering can cause contact dermatitis. Although an extremely uncomfortable skin condition, it is not a very serious one and is reversible when exposure stops. Nonetheless exposure to oils is widespread in the engineering industry and contact dermatitis arising from it is entirely foreseeable. Health surveillance would normally be required, but in this case could take the form of regular monthly skin inspections by a responsible person. This could be a foreman who has been trained in the recognition of dermatitis.

94   More information is contained in the booklet *Health surveillance under COSHH* (see References section).

Information, instruction and training for employees

95   This is a particularly important part of the management approach embodied in COSHH. Without the informed and competent participation of employees, any measures concluded in assessment are unlikely to be fully effective.

96   A properly informed and trained workforce is also better able to carry out COSHH action on its own initiative, thus allowing some of the load to be removed from management and supervisory staff.

97   COSHH requires that employees know:

- the risks to health created by exposure;
- the precautions which should be taken;

- results of any monitoring;

- collective results of any health surveillance.

98 The aim is to provide employees with information that is in a form most appropriate to their immediate needs. There is little point in providing huge amounts of intricately detailed technical information, but they should have access to more detailed information if required.

99 The extent of information, instruction and/or training that is required will be dependent on the nature of the individual situation. Where there are few employees working in inherently lower risk situations, the requirements can be met very simply. On the other hand, larger and more varied workforces, subject to greater risks, will require more attention for instruction information and training.

100 For employees who work under a minimum of supervision, the provision of suitable and sufficient information instruction and training is especially important. They need to be capable of evaluating and reacting correctly to exposure to hazardous substances on their own initiative: they cannot do this unless they have the necessary skills.

> An office typist is potentially exposed to solvent vapours from correction fluids and ozone generated by photocopiers. The risks are very low and compliance with simple instructions mounted on the photocopier and label recommendations on the correction fluid is all that is required.

> The emergency fire crew at an airport relies heavily on the use of self contained breathing apparatus (BA). Its effective operation and use is essential. Clearly all fire crew must have a thorough understanding of the risks involved as well as a high degree of competence in using BA properly. It is decided that all new staff will undergo immediate training on a recognised external course. The course is subject to examination and staff are employed on a probationary basis until they have satisfied the examiners. Subsequently firefighters all undergo annual refresher courses, also at external facilities, with report back from the course organisers on performance.

> An office cleaning contractor employs large numbers of relatively unskilled personnel. The staff work in teams of five late at night. Supervision is therefore limited. The employer attempts to control their exposure to hazardous substances by ensuring ready access to materials provided and assessed by him. Instructions are given to staff to use only those materials supplied by the contracting company and not cleaning materials found in the offices. There is a danger that inadvertent mixing of bleach and acid cleaners could produce chlorine. To decrease the likelihood of instructions being ignored, all staff are clearly informed of the potential risks involved in using unauthorised substances. Clear information and instruction is also given on where and how replacement materials can be obtained within the company; so that the need to use others is reduced.

28

Recording the assessment

Make a record of the assessment unless

101 It could very easily be repeated and explained at any time because it is simple and obvious, or the work is quite straightforward and low risk, is going to last only a very short time, and the time taken to write it down would be disproportionate.

> A supermarket employs late shifts of shelf packers, they handle bags of flour. In bakeries exposure to flour dust poses significant risk. During stacking, although the odd bag breaks, the amount of exposure is minimal and only lasts for a very short time. The risk to health is negligible and there is no point recording the matter in the assessment. On the other hand, the risks involved in handling damaged bleach containers are more serious. The assessment should note the necessary precautions, even if they are simply instructions for packers to leave damaged cartons untouched for safe removal by the shift supervisor.

Record sufficient information to ....

102 Show why decisions about risks and precautions have been arrived at. In particular, many of the requirements of COSHH are subject to the criteria of reasonable practicability. For instance, the use of personal protective equipment is only acceptable as an additional measure, if prevention or adequate control of exposure cannot be achieved reasonably practicably by other more effective means. If it has been decided that there will be reliance on PPE then the assessment should make it clear why other means were not considered feasible.

> Dangerous concentrations of toxic gases are very likely to be encountered in many confined spaces. Breathing apparatus will almost certainly be necessary if entry is attempted. It may be that some form of automatic cleaning system is available which could do away with the need for entry into the confined space. In that case assessment should show why it was not reasonably practicable to use that system rather than manned entry. It could be because the system is extremely expensive but the need for manned entry is rare. It could be that installation of the system would require widespread alteration to the whole premises, quite out of proportion to the benefits gained. But whatever the reason it should be made clear in the assessment.

103 Reflect the detail with which the assessment has been carried out.

> A medical research laboratory undertakes work on a vaccine for a poorly

understood exotic disease. The disease is known to be very infectious and a range of high standard control strategies is required. The assessment draws on a wide range of information sources, in order to achieve as much certainty as possible about the extent of risk and precautions required. The high risk also makes it important that all the measures are unambiguously stated so that confusion about what is to be done, why, who by, when etc is avoided. All this means that the assessment in these circumstances will be a detailed document.

A newly built large car factory regular conducts guided tours for the public. The tours are closely supervised by specialist public relations staff. The public, although in the factory, are not subject to the same level of risk as employees working full shifts. So while assessment for welders on the shop floor is conducted in some detail, for spectators on the other side of an enclosed viewing gallery the risk is minimal. Assessment for them might merely state that spectator exposure does not give rise to significant risk and normal supervision will ensure this remains the case. This does not mean to say that the public are never at significant risk. If the same factory conducted tours where the public went onto the shop floor, in closer contact with everything that goes on there, much more detailed consideration would be required.

104 Be useful and meaningful to those who will need to know about it, both now and in the future.

A plastic manufacturing process involves routine exposure to a hazardous substance for which no Maximum Exposure Limit or Occupational Exposure Standard has been set. In order to derive an in-house exposure limit, the company's occupational hygiene department collate technical literature and reach a decision on a working standard. Reproduction of all the technical literature in the assessment is of little use to those implementing the assessment conclusions. However, a summary of the reasons for choosing the particular standard will increase the likelihood that it is taken seriously.

A large oil refinery produces a very large and comprehensive assessment. The site employs a large workforce engaged in a wide variety of operations. In order to make sure that the assessment is easily accessible to all, it is produced in a modular form; broken down on the basis of different production and support processes. Different departments are provided only with the part of the assessment that is relevant to them, but they are made aware of the other parts and how to gain access to them. Each part of the assessment is carefully presented so that the main conclusions and recommendations appear at the beginning, with more detailed supporting information in separate annexes. In this way the crucial information which needs wider dissemination is 'up front' and more likely to be absorbed.

When the assessment needs to be reviewed

Think if and when the assessment needs to be reviewed

105   The assessment must in any case be reviewed at regular intervals and immediately if:

- there is any reason to suppose that the original assessment is no longer valid; or

- any of the circumstances of the work should change significantly.

106   The requirement is for review of the assessment. This does not mean that the whole assessment process will have to be repeated at each review. The first purpose of review is to see if the existing assessment is still suitable and sufficient. If it is, then it is not necessary to do any more.

107   If it appears that the assessment is no longer valid, it does not mean the whole assessment has to be revised. Only those parts of it that do not reflect the new situation need amendment.

108   Whether or not there is any real change in the situation there is an absolute requirement to review the situation on a **regular** basis. Without such discipline there is a real danger that gradual change over a period of time goes unnoticed and the previous assessment becomes unsuitable and insufficient by default.

109   The review interval is not specified in the Regulations but the Approved Code of Practice (see References section) recommends a period no longer than five years. Obviously the higher the potential risk and the greater the likelihood of change the shorter the review period should be.

110   The following are examples of changes which may make review necessary:

- volume of production;

> **A circuit board factory uses a solder bath process. To date fumes have been successfully extracted by local exhaust ventilation. Fulfilling a long term order will mean working two eight hour shifts instead of one. The ventilation equipment therefore has to work twice as long and new staff will have to be employed. Assessment review would probably indicate revised maintenance schedules for the ventilation equipment and would have to address the information, instruction and training needs of new personnel.**

- plant;

> A park maintenance department uses a number of knapsack sprayers for small scale application of pesticides. To reduce the amount of chemicals purchased it is decided to use ultra low volume, hand-held sprayers instead. Much smaller amounts of chemical are needed and this is likely to be an over-riding benefit with regard to COSHH compliance. However, the chemicals are used in more concentrated forms and there is some potential for increased spray drift. This also needs to be taken into account.

- materials;

> A car valetting specialist arranges with a commercial vehicle dealer to clean the cabs of lorries. The way he uses substances is much the same as for cars, but much heavier duty cleaning materials are required. The assessment will need to take into account the new substances involved.

- process;

> A toy factory paints components by means of a production line passing through a paint bath. To improve finish quality and reduce paint wastage it is replaced by a spraying assembly. There is an obvious increase in the amount of vapour generated which requires assessment.

- control methods (COSHH requires that wherever it is reasonably practicable the most inherently effective methods of exposure prevention or control should be used. As the range of methods improves and expands it becomes more reasonably practicable to use them.)

> A quarry installs a new rock crushing plant. One of the benefits of this is that it is designed to limit the generation and spread of dust. At first sight this appears to reduce the need for an existing reliance on respirators but the new equipment is subject to heavy wear and tear. Assessment will need to consider the maintenance needs of the new plant to sustain its dust suppression capabilities and to what extent respirators can be dispensed with in light of realistic levels of exposure.

111 Also be alert for need to review if, for example:

- ill health related to work is reported;

- there is new evidence about hazards of substances;

- monitoring or health surveillance results show any loss of control;

- new or improved techniques of control become reasonably practicable.

Competence

Introduction

112 Other parts of this booklet explain what needs to go into a 'suitable and sufficient' assessment. This part of the booklet is intended to help employers decide who should carry out the assessment.

113 COSHH does not aim to transform employers and their staff into expert occupational hygienists. Many assessments will be more complicated and require more sophisticated technical input: but the aim is always to devise measures that will work in the real circumstances. That is dependent on a thorough appreciation of what happens in real life and it is employers and their staff who know that best. For this reason assessment should always be started 'in house'.

114 Employers may carry out the tasks themselves or they may delegate them to other people in the organisation or they may call in expertise from outside. The decision as to which course of action to take (or any combination of these) should depend on the knowledge and experience needed for the particular job in hand. Regulation 12(3) states that any person who does any work in connection with the employer's duties under COSHH must have the necessary information, instruction and training.

115 The possession of qualifications in occupational hygiene or membership of relevant professional bodies is an important indicator (but not guarantee) of competence; especially where situations require higher levels of skill. However, formal qualifications are not the only ones that are relevant. Practical experience of likely circumstances is important, as is training in principles of occupational hygiene that does not lead to formal qualifications. Such qualifications are more likely to be appropriate for 'in-house' assessment of less technically demanding risks.

116 People carrying out assessments and consequential tasks must be given the necessary facilities and authority to do the work competently. They need to have enough time and status to gather the information, talk to the appropriate people, look at any existing records and examine the workplace. A number of different people may be assigned different tasks within the assessment, but there must be reporting arrangements so that their findings are brought quickly to the attention of the employer or to some other specially delegated representative of the employer who can coordinate the conclusions and can directly authorise any necessary action.

117 More specific guidance may be available from industry associations about the sorts of people who are most likely to be able to help with assessments and other duties under

COSHH where the expertise does not exist within the undertaking. In such situations, the use of outside consultants may often be cost-effective, enabling the work to be carried out quickly and to a high standard.

What are the basic skills for someone doing an assessment?

118 Whoever carries out the assessment, whether the employer or someone else delegated to lead or do it, that person should have the abilities set out in the following paragraphs. How extensive those abilities need to be depends on the individual situation. As the complexity or severity of the risk increases so does the need for more able assessors.

Understand the basic requirements of the Regulations

119 This is not a need for a legalistic skill, but an understanding of the point of each regulation and what it involves. (The person should also have read and understood the Approved Codes of Practice and relevant guidance.)

Gather relevant information about exposures and risks systematically

120 The information required calls for abilities to:

- observe, in order to really appreciate what is going on and the significance of what they see, particularly if it diverges from written procedures;

- predict possible departures from observed practice and realise their significance;

- ask relevant questions of supervisors, managers, employers, advisers etc and realise the implications of the responses. Also, if relevant, being able to undertake simple diagnostic tests;

- identify and review any relevant technical literature;

- draw all the information together in a systematic way, to estimate likelihoods and consequences;

- form valid and justifiable conclusions about exposures and risks.

Specify the steps to be taken to comply with the Regulations

121 This involves:

- pursuing fundamental questions about whether there is a need for any exposures to occur;

- having an appreciation of the range of possible control measures and the measures to sustain control, and the relative reliability of each;

- being able to look critically at existing arrangements; and

- being able to identify in broad terms the types of changes needed. (Certain aspects may then need to be referred to relevant specialists.)

Understand their own limitations

122 The person must know or be made aware of the areas of expertise that might need to be involved in an assessment and at what stage to call upon the knowledge and skills of others. For example, air sampling should only be carried out by people who have been trained in the techniques and procedures, and the planning of a monitoring strategy requires a fairly high level of professional training.

123 Where respiratory protective equipment is being used, someone with a sound knowledge of occupational hygiene principles as well as the real procedures and practices should be involved. This is because of the need for precision about the risks and the need to look for possible alternative methods of control.

Make a report

124 The person must be able to communicate their findings about the risks and precautions to the employer and to other people who need to know, whether the report is oral or written.

Engaging expertise from outside the organisation

125 More detailed guidance on the selection and use of consultants is contained in the HSE booklet *Selecting a Health and Safety consultancy*. This describes professional capabilities that can usually be expected from health and safety consultants. It also sets out the questions to ask consultants, to select one with the appropriate qualifications for the job in hand.

126 Employers should ensure that they cannot do the work themselves before opting to use consultants. Where consultants are used the main criteria are to:

- make sure you and the consultants know exactly what they are being employed to do;

- work with the consultants rather than leaving them to do the task in isolation;

- act on the recommendations proposed.

Reasonable practicability

127 A number of COSHH requirements are subject to reasonable practicability. They are:

Regulation 3(1). The extension of duties for the benefit of non-employees;

Regulation 7(1). The duty to prevent exposure to hazardous substances;

Regulation 7(2). The duty to use control measures other than personal protective equipment;

Regulation 7(3). The duty to control exposure to carcinogens by specific measures for example, by total enclosure;

Regulation 7(6). The duty to reduce exposure below the specified level for Maximum Exposure Limit substances;

Regulation 7(7). For Occupational Exposure Standard substances the duty to recognise and rectify excursions above the set limit.

128 Reasonably practicable has a specific meaning in law outlined below. However, deciding what is or is not reasonably practicable depends on individual circumstances and cannot be subjected to standard formulae.

129 Reasonable practicability is essentially a matter of balancing the degree of risk against the time, trouble, cost and physical difficulty of the measures necessary to avoid it. Clearly the greater the risk the more reasonable it is to do something about it; and vice versa. It is important to remember that the judgement is driven by the risk and **not** the size or financial position of the employer concerned.

130 Finding the balance is a matter of judgement. It fits well with assessment which is above all a matter of informed judgement. Where decisions for compliance with COSHH are subject to reasonable practicability, then the assessment should indicate why a particular decision has been made.

131 There are various sources of information and indicators to aid decisions on reasonable practicability.

- HSE codes and guidance.

- Industry body guidance.

- Accepted good practice (but this may not necessarily be the same as usual practice).

- If something can be done that can be a good starting point in deciding whether it is reasonably practical.

- The recommendations of manufacturers and suppliers.

- The hazardous nature of the substance involved and the risk it presents, both of which will be clear if the earlier stages of assessment are suitable and sufficient.

Duties towards non-employees

A car spraying business uses twin pack isocyanate paints which are known to be very potent sensitising agents. The business is sited on a small industrial estate and backs onto a primary school on the other side of a high brick wall. The standards of control for spray operators is of the highest order and fully complies with COSHH. Controls involve use of local exhaust ventilation. This has to vent somewhere and special precautions will be required to ensure that isocyanates do not drift into the school playground. If the business had been sited in isolated rural premises then the likelihood of public exposure would be vastly reduced and precautions for their benefit would not be so reasonably practicable.

Prevention of exposure

A national house-building company uses an organic solvent to clean floor tiles after walls and ceilings have been decorated. Cleaning the tiles involves manual application of the solvent with potential for heavy exposure. Exposure can be prevented by laying floor tiles after painting the walls and ceilings so that the need for any cleaning is done away with completely. This is a very simple measure, easy to implement and sustain, with the added benefit of no extra cost. At the same time it removes a significant risk to health and thus the minor change can be considered reasonably practicable.

At a major international airport, diesel powered tugs are used to move aircraft into maintenance hangars. There has been some concern about exposure to diesel fumes in the hangar. It has been suggested that only electrically powered vehicles should be used inside the building. To do so would effectively require doubling the number of tugs with one electric vehicle for each diesel one. A substantial battery charging infrastructure would have to be installed. Battery charging in itself introduces explosion risks and exposure to hazardous substances. The system of work would also involve an extra process as the diesel tugs are unhitched and the electric ones hitched and vice versa. This would also introduce new risks. Fume generation in the hangar is brief as the tugs only enter when they are parking the aircraft and do not idle when inside. Because of their essential operational role tugs are subject to rigorous maintenance and excessive emissions from poorly maintained engines are rare, as are emissions arising from worn pumps and injectors. There is good natural ventilation because of the large doors and this is supplemented by ventilation fans. In these circumstances the benefits of using electric powered vehicles appear outweighed, not only because of the additional resource and effort required, but also because of the new risks that would be introduced. The option would appear not to be reasonably practicable.

Methods for controlling exposure

In analytical work a chemical plant laboratory has to use a powdered reagent which is very toxic. During weighing dust is liberated and this is removed by local exhaust ventilation inside a sealed enclosure. However, much more reliable control can be achieved by avoiding dust generation in the first place. Although more expensive, the substance is available in tablet form. The tablet form does not significantly alter the validity of test results or the procedure that is used. In view of the extremely toxic nature of the substance, the elimination (or at least strict minimisation) of exposure to it is a high priority. By itself this justifies the extra expense of the tablet form and in this example the case is further strengthened by the fact that using it does not involve difficult change to the test procedure.

A specialist roadmarking contractor uses a high pressure compressed air technique. The paint used contains solvents which are inevitably liberated in substantial concentrations. No alternative paint is available and so adequate control of exposure to this particular substance must be achieved. At present control relies heavily on respirators and protective clothing. Because of the high concentrations encountered it is unlikely that this will be consistently effective. There is also reluctance amongst employees to wear the protective equipment. There are alternative techniques available that do not entail high pressure air. They are slightly slower than the existing method, but they drastically reduce the emission of vapour, and consequently employee exposure. As it wears out, it would seem reasonably practicable to progressively replace existing equipment with the alternative. Even if it could be shown that this is not a reasonable proposal (but there would have to be good reason and cost alone is unlikely to be sufficient), then that does not mean personal protection can remain as the only control. Other options more effective than PPE might include modification of the existing equipment so that it does not liberate so much vapour, eg shrouded nozzles and solvent recovery circuits.

132 Although personal protective equipment should be seen as an additional last resort there are many occasions where its use cannot be avoided. However, assessment should still show why it was not reasonably practicable to achieve control without resorting to personal protection.

A dairy company runs a large number of electric milk floats. Battery maintenance inevitably involves potential exposure to concentrated sulphuric acid. Gloves, apron and a faceshield are used. In assessment the feasibility of a system of work removing the need to handle acid containers manually is considered. A reliable automated system would, in practice, be extremely difficult to develop, complicated to operate and maintain and may well not reduce the potential for exposure as much as planned. For instance, complex systems are more prone to breakdown and repair crews would then be exposed to the acid at close quarters more frequently. In these circumstances, installing an automated system would not seem to be a reasonably practicable option. On the other hand, the likelihood of spillage during manual handling can be reduced by using better designed containers. Introducing these is a simple matter and can be considered reasonably practicable, although it does not remove the need for protective clothing.

Control of exposure below the maximum exposure limit

A foundry workshop has an existing ventilation system for removing silica dust, during separation of moulds and castings. It consists of an open 'knocking out' platform behind which is situated an exhaust inlet. Monitoring has shown that exposure is controlled to the MEL level although not greatly reduced below it. However, to assess compliance with control of exposure to silica, consideration of the reasonable practicability of additional reduction of exposure is needed. The installation is in daily use by a number of different workers. Since exposure is only marginally below the MEL limit, comparatively minor faults in the system will easily result in over-exposure. Those faults may well have to wait until the next examination before they come to light. In short there is very little margin for error. The effectiveness of the existing equipment can be significantly improved by installing side enclosures. They are easily and cheaply installed and can be designed so that they do not hinder access. (Experience has shown that well designed systems can reduce exposure to about 0.1 mg/m^3 when the MEL limit is 0.3). In these circumstances they are a reasonably practicable addition to the existing control measures.

Recognition of and reaction to excursions above occupational exposure standards.

It is important to remember that the Regulations require that excursions are both identified and controlled as soon as is reasonably practicable. The aim is not merely to react quickly to excursions when employers become aware of them, but also to identify quickly that there has been an excursion when it happens.

Ethanol is a widely used industrial feedstock and exposure may be encountered in many workplaces. It has an occupational exposure standard (OES) and failure of control measures could result in excursions above it. It is not a strong smelling substance and therefore the excursion may not be immediately apparent. In order to ensure that excursions are identified quickly, employees are informed of the likely indicators and instructed to tell their supervisor if they notice any of them. In addition, because of uncertainty about exposure levels, a monitoring programme is established to help detect excursions. If excessive exposure is then identified adequate control must be regained quickly. This will require in particular the resources and authority for relevant personnel to identify the causes and repair the shortcomings. Respiratory protective equipment may be temporarily required, to reduce exposure below the OES while repairs are effected. (Investigation may well indicate that initial assessment conclusions need to be revised.)

References

A brief summary and explanation of COSHH is contained in the following leaflet, obtainable free from HSE Books:

COSHH - The new brief guide for employers HSE Books 1999 INDG136

The following publications give more detailed information:

Codes of Practice

General COSHH ACOP and Carcinogens ACOP and Biological agents ACOP (including the Control of Substances Hazardous to Health Regulations 1999) L5 HSE Books 1999
  ISBN 0 7176 1670 3

COSHH Essentials: Easy steps to control chemicals HSG193 HSE Books 1999
  ISBN 0 7176 2421 8 (see note overleaf)

Control of Substances Hazardous to Health in Fumigation Operations; Approved Code of Practice L86 HSE Books 1996
  ISBN 0 7176 1195 7

Consolidation of COSHH in the potteries *Control of Substances Hazardous to Health in the production of pottery* Approved Code of Practice L60 HSE Books 1998
  ISBN 0 7176 0849 2

The prevention or control of legionellosis (including legionnaires' disease) L8 HSE Books 1995
  ISBN 0 7176 0732 1

Safe use of pesticides for non-agricultural purposes L9 HSE Books 1995
  ISBN 0 7176 0542 6

Other HSE Guidance

COSHH: An Open Learning Course HSE Books 1995
  ISBN 0 7176 0850 6

EH40/99, *Occupational Exposure Limits* (containing the list of occupational exposure standards for use with the Control of Substances Hazardous to Health Regulations) HSE Books 1999
  ISBN 0 7176 1660 6

EH 44, *Dust: General Principles of Protection* (rev) HSE Books 1997
  ISBN 0 7176 1435 2

MS 24, *Medical aspects of Occupational Skin Disease* HSE Books 1998
  ISBN 0 7176 1545 6

HSG37, *An Introduction to Local Exhaust Ventilation* HSE Books 1993
ISBN 0 7176 1001 2

HSG53, *The selection, use and maintenance of respiratory protective equipment - a Practical Guide* HSE Books 1998
ISBN 0 7176 1537 5

HSG65, *Successful Health and Safety Management* HSE Books 1997
ISBN 0 7176 1276 7

HSG54, *The Maintenance, examination and testing of Local Exhaust Ventilation* HSE Books 1998
ISBN 0 7176 1485 9

Health surveillance under COSHH - guidance for employers HSE Books 1990
ISBN 0 7176 0491 8

HSG110, *Seven Steps to successful substitution of hazardous substances* HSE Books 1994
ISBN 0 7176 0695 3

HSG173, *Monitoring strategies for toxic substances* HSE Books 1997
ISBN 0 7176 1411 5

Selecting a Health and Safety consultancy HSE Books 1992 INDG133

Read the label: How to find out if chemicals are dangerous HSE Books 1995 INDG186

Consulting employees on health and safety: a guide to the law HSE Books 1996 INDG232

All the above is HSE guidance that is relevant to a wide variety of different work activities. There is a great deal more material, both from HSE and other organisations, giving guidance more specific to particular sectors.

Note: COSHH essentials: Easy steps to control chemicals has been produced since the publication of *A step by step guide to COSHH assessment*. It uses a simple checklist approach to help firms (particularly small firms) cut through the complexity of assessing the risks associated with working with chemicals and identify action to protect workers. It contains illustrated guidance sheets for suitable controls for common tasks, for example, mixing and weighing. It does not cover non-routine operations, process fumes or dusts, biological agents and substances needing special control measures (eg where the health risk is cancer or asthma).

A step by step guide to COSHH assessment still remains valid where the new *COSHH essentials: Easy steps to control chemicals* does not apply, for example, for non-routine operations, process fumes or dusts, biological agents and substances which can cause cancer or asthma.

Printed and published by the Health and Safety Executive C75 11/99